Pope Leo XIV

The First American Pope

by Grace Hansen

Abdo Kids Jumbo is an Imprint of Abdo Kids
abdobooks.com

abdobooks.com

Published by Abdo Kids, a division of ABDO, PO Box 398166, Minneapolis, Minnesota 55439.

Printed in the United States of America, North Mankato, Minnesota.

052025

092025

Photo Credits: Alamy, Getty Images, Shutterstock,
©Caitriana Nicholson p.9/CC BY-SA 2.0, ©Galería fotográfica PCM, Perú p.13/CC BY-NC-SA 2.0,

Production Contributors: Teddy Borth, Jennie Forsberg, Grace Hansen

Design Contributors: Candice Keimig, Pakou Moua

Library of Congress Control Number: 2025938854

Publisher's Cataloging-in-Publication Data

Names: Hansen, Grace, author.

Title: Pope Leo XIV: the first American pope / by Grace Hansen

Description: Minneapolis, Minnesota : Abdo Kids, 2026 | Series: History maker biographies | Includes online resources and index.

Identifiers: ISBN 9798384908685 (lib. bdg.) | ISBN 9798384908722 (ebook) | ISBN 9798384908746 (read-to-me ebook)

Subjects: LCSH: Leo XIV, Pope, 1955---Juvenile literature. | Prevost, Robert Francis, 1955---Juvenile literature. | Catholic Church--History--21st century--Juvenile literature. | Religious leaders--Juvenile literature. | Popes--Juvenile literature. | Papal conclaves--Juvenile literature.

Classification: DDC 282.092--dc23

Table of Contents

Early Years 4

Education 8

Priesthood and Missionary Work 12

The Path to Popehood 16

Pope Leo XIV 18

Timeline. 22

Glossary 23

Index 24

Abdo Kids Code. 24

Early Years

Robert Francis Prevost was born on September 14, 1955, in Chicago, Illinois. He lived with his parents and two older brothers. His family saw something special in him from a young age.

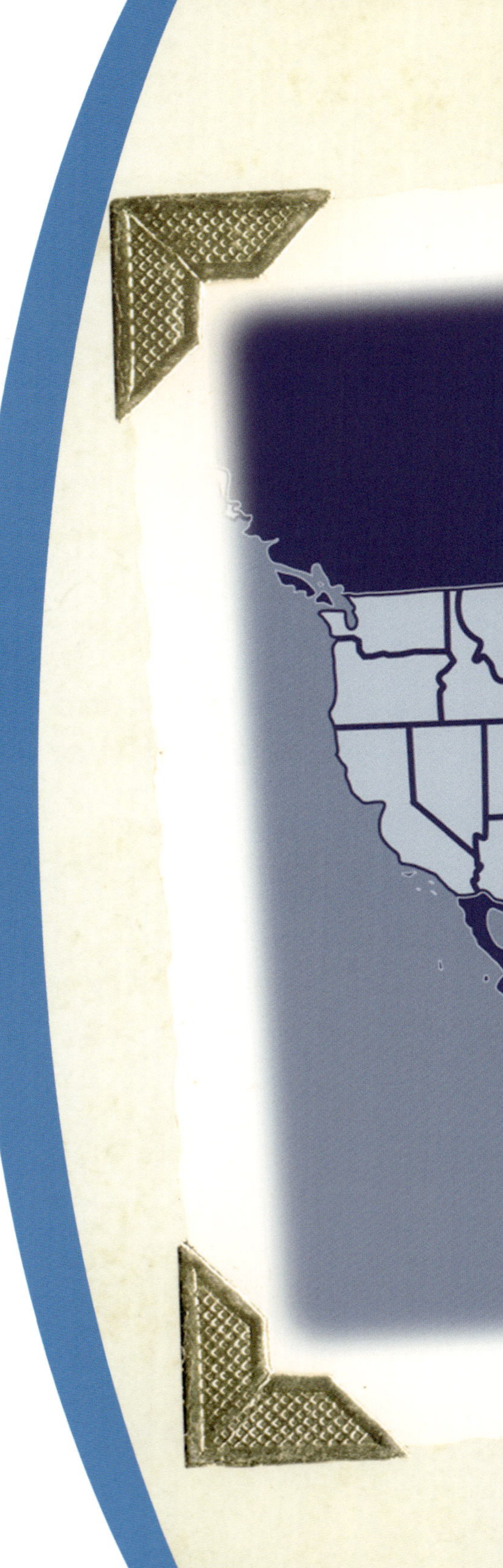

Chicago,
Illinois

Robert grew up in Dolton, Illinois. He knew early on that he wanted to be a priest. Robert went to school at St. Mary of the Assumption. He served as an **altar boy** and sang in the church choir.

Robert's childhood home

Education

Robert went to high school in Holland, Michigan. It was a special school for young men who wanted to be Catholic priests. Robert was a very good student and did many activities, including speech and debate.

St. Augustine Seminary High School

Robert went on to attend college at Villanova University in Pennsylvania. There, he earned a degree in math. He returned to Chicago to receive his **theological** education. He then went on to study in Rome, Italy.

CAMPUS MINISTRY
CAMPUS
MINISTRY
OFFICE

Priesthood and Missionary Work

Robert was **ordained** a priest on June 19, 1982, in Rome. In 1985, Father Prevost left for Chulucanas, Peru, to join the **Augustinian mission**. At the same time, he studied for his **doctoral** degree, which he earned in 1987.

Chulucanas, Peru

Pope John Paul II

In 1988, Father Prevost again joined the **Augustinian mission** in Peru. He served the community in Trujillo for more than 10 years. In 1999, he returned to Chicago for an important role at an Augustinian church.

Prevost's room in the Augustine convent in Trujillo

The Path to Popehood

In November 2015, Pope Francis named Prevost **Bishop** of Chiclayo, Peru. Prevost served in this role until 2023. Pope Francis then moved him to Rome to help manage bishops around the world. He also made Prevost a **cardinal**.

Pope
Francis

Pope Leo XIV

In 2025, Pope Francis died. Catholics and other people around the world were very sad. But the church had to choose a new pope. The **cardinals** came together to vote.

Just 33 hours later, on May 8, it was decided. Prevost would become the 267th leader of the Roman Catholic Church. People thought he would be a good and **unifying** leader, like Francis. Prevost would be known as Pope Leo XIV.

Timeline

1955
September 14
Robert Francis Prevost is born in Chicago, Illinois. He grows up near the South Side of Chicago in Dolton.

1969
Robert attends St. Augustine Seminary High School in Holland, Michigan.

1977
Robert graduates from Villanova University in Pennsylvania.

1982
June 19
Robert is made a priest.

1985
Father Prevost joins the **Augustinian mission** in Chulucanas, Peru.

1988
Father Prevost returns to the Augustinian mission, but in Trujillo, Peru. He serves the community there for more than 10 years.

2015
Pope Francis names Prevost as **Bishop** of Chiclayo, Peru. He remains in this role until Pope Francis asks him to come to Rome.

2023
September 30
Pope Francis makes Prevost a **cardinal**.

2025
May 8
Prevost is elected to be the 267th pope. He chooses the name Pope Leo XIV.

Glossary

altar boy – a young male person who assists the clergy in religious services.

Augustinian – of or relating to a religious order whose members follow the Rule of Saint Augustine.

bishop – in the Catholic Church, a leader who is above a priest, but below an archbishop and a cardinal.

cardinal – a high official of the Roman Catholic Church who is chosen by the pope.

doctoral – the degree, title, or rank of a doctor. Prevost is a doctor of canon law, which is the code of laws that the Catholic Church follows.

mission – a place, usually in a city, that provides things like food, clothing, or a place to sleep to the poor, and is typically operated by a church.

ordained – made a Christian minister or priest by a special ceremony.

theological – relating to theology, which is the study of religion.

unifying – bringing together.

Index

bishop 16

cardinal 16

Chicago, Illinois 4, 10, 14

Chiclayo, Peru 16

Chulucanas, Peru 12

Dolton, Illinois 6

family 4

Holland, Michigan 8

Pennsylvania 10

Pope Francis 16, 18, 20

priesthood 12, 14

Rome, Italy 10, 12, 16

St. Mary of the Assumption 6

Trujillo, Peru 14

Villanova University 10

Visit **abdokids.com** to access crafts, games, videos, and more!

Use Abdo Kids code

HPK8685

or scan this QR code!